CHILDREN OF THE STARS

Other Books by Freddie Langeler

Children of the Earth

Fairies

For information, write to Kabouter Products,
1241 21st Street, Oakland, CA 94607.USA

Text: Annemarie Dragt and Dagmar Traub
ISBN 1-56937-100-8
Library of Congress Catalog Number: 95-83108

Printed in Hong Kong

CHILDREN OF THE STARS

By

Freddie Langeler

Kabouter Products

As children on earth are going to bed,
The moon sticks out her yellow head.
The children of the stars appear
And light their lanterns, bright and clear.

Out from the darkness, one by one,
The stars come forth; night has begun.
Thousands of them: see how they shimmer,
And fill the sky with shiny glimmer.

Two starry horses pull a cart,
Star children walk with happy heart.
They are playing, yet they have an aim,
'Cover the sky with light' is the game.

Who's riding in that carriage so gay?
Prince or princess, elf or fay?
The moon, with most awesome glow of all,
Guides from the distance with silent call.

See in the clouds, a starship sailing
The boatsman looks out past the railing.
Observes with great curiosity—
Something is drifting—what could it be?

The clouds float silently through space,
High up above, a quiet place.
The rain they bring will help the earth
To give to nature a fresh, new birth.

Two little star boys from afar,
Go fishing with a golden star.
The silver fish swim near the light;
The boys enjoy a sparkling sight!

Big Dipper, North Star, Orion's Sword,
Clusters of stars have been adored.
Leo, the Lion, and Lepus, the Hare,
Shining so clear, bring light everywhere.

Starchildren, Starchildren, who is there?
It is friend Whitecoat, the Polar bear.
Two shining star girls riding high,
Make Whitecoat's favorite night in the sky!

Each of the stars has a wonderful story,
Full of adventure, telling of glory.
How stars helped people on earth to see,
Travel by dark, and predict what would be.

O look! What is happening? Tell me, quick!

They're falling down! Why? Are they sick?

A blazing big star is shooting through:

Makes the stars topple, and frightens them, too.

Something wondrous is dashing through space.

A cheerful smile on the little boy's face.

The stars are falling from the sky,

"Let's visit earth!" they joyously cry.

Starchildren hold each other's hands,

While travelling through these unknown lands.

But look, the moon makes an angry face:

"Go home now quickly, away from this place!"

Moon's watching to keep the sky in order.

From heaven to earth, stars crossed the border.

Star children on earth for the very first time—

But their home is above; so back they must climb.

"Careful, careful, don't be loud.
See the gateway in this cloud?
Here is where you have to go.
Your time is up, the sun will show!"

"Starchildren, you have fallen so deep
The world down here is still asleep.
If the day wakes up and you're still here,
Your light will go out!" Now the moon is severe.

The moon peeks through the window cloud,
Welcoming back the adventurous crowd.
They scrub and clean and polish their light,
To make it shine and shimmer all night.

You children of light! You have such fun!
Don't you know it's late, almost time for the sun?
Yet the moon looks friendly and smiles as you play—
Are you a dream? Are you real? Who's to say?

They are going to bed, soon off to sleep,

To dream of adventure, and of falling so deep.

They have done their work and feel content.

Now the children on earth, with merriment

Are the light of the day; they sing and play.

When the evening comes, the sun will set,

The children of earth will go to bed.

When all of the world is enveloped in dark,

The stars will bring light, full of glimmer and spark.

Freddie Langeler was a well-known Dutch illustrator in the 1920's. From 1913 on, Freddie Langeler worked regularly for Uitgeverij Kluitman in the Netherlands. She illustrated many children's books, some of which became classics and are enjoyed by children up to the present day. This is the first time that Langeler's work is published in the United States.